Messages from the Enochian Tablets

A LIGHTWORKER'S GUIDE TO ENERGETIC CLEARING

Ways to Accelerate Your Spiritual Path
Channeled Writings and Healing Symbols
Higher Vibrations of Crystals
Pendulum Energy Reading System
Intuitive Healing Methods
Deactivation Codes

Diana Kushenbach

BALBOA
PRESS

A DIVISION OF HAY HOUSE

Copyright © 2013 Diana Kushenbach.

All rights reserved. No part of this book may be used or reproduced by any means, graphic, electronic, or mechanical, including photocopying, recording, taping or by any information storage retrieval system without the written permission of the publisher except in the case of brief quotations embodied in critical articles and reviews.

Messages from the Enochian Tablets & A Lightworker's Guide to Energetic Clearing was written to share information from guidance received intuitively by the author. "Healing" in this book relates to clearing and balancing energies. This information is not to be used as an alternative to seeking qualified doctors or professionals for medical or mental health issues.

Balboa Press books may be ordered through booksellers or by contacting:
Balboa Press
A Division of Hay House
1663 Liberty Drive
Bloomington, IN 47403
www.balboapress.com
1-(877) 407-4847

Because of the dynamic nature of the Internet, any web addresses or links contained in this book may have changed since publication and may no longer be valid. The views expressed in this work are solely those of the author and do not necessarily reflect the views of the publisher, and the publisher hereby disclaims any responsibility for them.

The author of this book does not dispense medical advice or prescribe the use of any technique as a form of treatment for physical, emotional, or medical problems without the advice of a physician, either directly or indirectly. The intent of the author is only to offer information of a general nature to help you in your quest for emotional and spiritual well-being. In the event you use any of the information in this book for yourself, which is your constitutional right, the author and the publisher assume no responsibility for your actions.

Any people depicted in stock imagery provided by Thinkstock are models, and such images are being used for illustrative purposes only.
Certain stock imagery © Thinkstock.

Printed in the United States of America.

ISBN: 978-1-4525-7808-8 (sc)
ISBN: 978-1-4525-7809-5 (e)
Library of Congress Control Number: 2013912893

Balboa Press rev. date: 7/19/2013

I give special thanks to my husband Christopher and my dear friend Pat for experiencing this journey with me.

Table of Contents

Introduction ix

Part I - Messages from the Enochian Tablets

The Purpose of the Enochian Tablets..................... 1
Vow to Protect the Children of God 1
History of Creation 2
Why Did God's Son Luciferis Leave Heaven? 5
The Universal Truth 7
Heaven's Gates 9
Why God Added Man 9
Original Sin and God's Response 10
Who is the Son of Jehovah? 11
Seven Ways to Overpower Satan 12
Stopping the Spread of Evil 14
Free Will 16

Part II - A Lightworker's Guide to Energetic Healing

My Cup Overflows...................................... 20
A Flower Unfolding..................................... 21
Even Though I Walk Through the Darkest Valley,
    I Fear No Evil 22

He Leads Me in Right Paths 23
December 21, 2012 24
Alignment Perceived 25
Who Are You Channeling? 26
Reach Higher for Your Guidance 28
Getting Your Signals................................ 29
How Energies Get into the Energy Field............... 30
Mediumship and Healing............................ 32
Intuitive Crystal Healing 35
   Raising the Vibration of Crystals........................38
   Applications for Crystals Raised to Higher Vibration.......39
   Crystal Removal Tools for Energetic Parasites
      and Other Debris 47
Pendulum Healing—A Multi-Purpose Method
   for Reading Energy 47
My Experiences with Problematic Energies 54
   Psychic Children 56
   Energy Vampires......................................61
   Stealing Someone's Spiritual Destiny 62
   Curses and Intentions..................................64
Enochian Healing and Removal Symbols 65
Deactivation Codes 69
Testimonials 71

Introduction

I'm going to begin creating a new paradigm by lowering your instinct. What this means is that I open your mind to possibilities that you previously have not discovered. These possibilities extend beyond your limiting beliefs to a new understanding and make a shift in your free-thinking mind. Limiting beliefs restrict your ability to succeed in new areas of growth. Now, instead of believing that just one way exists, we open your mind to a very powerful energy, which lowers your instinct and allows for a new paradigm to begin. Take a moment to breathe in this new energy and new paradigm.

Do you believe that you are ready to open your access to psychic abilities? Lower your instinct about the words psychic, gypsy, crystal balls, and limiting beliefs about psychics in general. Create a new paradigm that allows for new possibilities. It is OK to still be skeptical.

I opened up to having psychic abilities after my best friend, Barbra, died suddenly and unexpectedly from pneumonia at age thirty-six. We had been close friends since grade school. The shock of a sudden life change is what opened my abilities. I found myself aware of her presence after she passed, and I wanted to know more. Two days after she died, a high-profile missing person case, where I knew the people involved, was all over the news. I suddenly felt the need to learn how to communicate with someone who was no longer in this physical existence. I read whatever information I could find on the Internet and started taking local mediumship classes. I went to a psychic for a reading and started connecting with like-minded people. I had the drive to keep learning.

Information started coming in for me in various ways. I would have as many as three dreams per night detailing crimes and locations of evidence. Even though I didn't know how or why this information was coming in, I wrote it all down, including dates, times, and phone numbers. I even had one visit from Barbra. Getting better at understanding what was happening with me, I started trying to use what I had learned to help with missing person cases. I spent months trying to locate the victims, since I believed that was all that I could do to help. I began to notice a very strong competitive nature among other psychics who were doing the same thing. If I felt the need to contact police, I did it anonymously. I realized that in my previous career in law enforcement, I would have thought that someone like me giving psychic information about a case was crazy. What would an Investigator do with information that was so vague? I submitted it anyway.

I have become a very clear channel for God/Source to speak through me and give messages to those who need to hear from loved ones on the other side, to help them heal themselves, and to bring out their own personal truth. I am able to hear God/Source instructions for each person's situation, since there isn't one answer that fits all. I focus on assisting people with their connection so that they can receive the highest guidance and have their own God/Source conversation without my help. When working with students, my motto has always been, "I want you to be better than I am." This adventure is not just about what I want and receiving it the way I ask. The larger purpose is the reason I came to this planet—an ongoing process made up of layers, each built upon the last, changing the idea of "what is and will be," hundreds of times. We call this growth.

I was not aware that there were Enochian Tablets until I started channeling from my spiritual destiny. I was told that to be able to remember their own purpose certain people needed the information that I was writing. The second part of this book, *A Lightworker's Guide to Energetic Healing*, is based on my experiences. Because I receive this information does not mean that I understand it all, but I can feel energetically that it works.

I hope that you enjoy the parts that were meant for you to read and perhaps share with others. I thank God, my family, and close friends for all of the love and support they have given my path and will continue to give in the future.

Part I - Messages from the Enochian Tablets

The Purpose of the Enochian Tablets

When God first spoke to the Angels, he created the Enochian Tablets to explain the duties of the Angels. Over time this Tablet became a manuscript on how to better serve God and his plan for "all that is, was, and will be." The details contained within this series of manuscripts have been previously isolated from man in order to keep them sacred. It is at this time that permission has been granted to share certain passages with man in order for him to experience the truth from a different perspective. Several previous versions of this Tablet have been written in different languages, none of them containing completely factual information. Things that have been written over the ages are not necessarily as they seem to be in many versions of God's word. Believe as you may and judge with your soul as to the authenticity of any writing. That is when you will know what you believe.

How to Protect the Children of God

1. Each Angel shall use its service to free the children of God from any harm.

2. No Angel shall provide its own truth before that of God.
3. Angels must uphold the right to Free Will.
4. The innocent will not be bound by the rules of the wicked.
5. Angels may not interfere in common man's experiences.
6. The souls of the lost will be collected and restored.
7. No proof of Angels will ever be seen.
8. Angels may not disobey God.
9. God can free the tortured souls of the wicked.
10. Angels may use the power of the sword to kill the wicked.
11. God will banish disobedient Angels for life.
12. Angels who use their power to disobey will be killed.

History of Creation

When creation started, there was a spark of Light that created more sparks and then a large ball of fire. Within every spark there was life. Life continued to grow and still does. As the fire burns, we observe the power of this life force. Every ember connects to the whole until it yields the entire universe and beyond. Unseen layers exist and more are created each day. This way of life yields peace and freedom with all parts co-existing for this purpose. The Temple of Creation, which we call God, is where the first spark was created. Within the stillness of this peace was a co-creation that was not as strong as the Temple and sought to be the Temple. This was the first act of freedom. The Temple was not in balance with the universe, and the ember that sought the Temple fell to Earth. This fallen ember is Luciferis, who continued to seek the Temple from a place far from creation. He chose to fall instead of igniting new layers of life force. Before he fell, Luciferis told God that He would never be able to stop him or change him. This discourse could be felt in every place in time and after, and soon the balance of the universe was no longer.

Many thousands of years passed before the folly of the Earth erupted into pain and death. All of God's creatures were bitten by Luciferis until there were none. This was the end of man on Earth. Briefly there was silence, and the waters cleared to ignite yet another spark of creation: God's team of protectors of man, the Angels. Without man, the universe would be no more, as these parts of the Temple existed to grow a new focus of love. In order for the new love to survive, a congregation of Angels, called the Archangels, entered into Earth. These Angels were supreme beings whose focus was to light up the Earth, the way it had once been, and to free the humans from the enslavement of Luciferis and the fallen.

God sent a son to spark creation once again. This son was Jesibel, who entered into Earth life shortly after the planet was extinct. The son Jesibel was cautioned not to join Luciferis, but he did not heed God's warning and was killed by the Archangels. Years went on before the Archangels made headway. Man no longer felt the Temple, as Luciferis prevented this from happening. Luciferis began to assemble an army of his own. He solicited many to be his soldiers by playing on their fear that history would repeat itself and that the Temple was not strong enough to protect them. The battles involving God, man, and wicked continued throughout the endless days of the demise of man.

A third spark ignited, and a congregation of higher beings of Light connected with the Temple and the Archangels. They were called "The Protectors of the Light." All found purpose in preserving the integrity of the universe and the Temple and eliminating soldiers of the fallen. The Earth was to be restored to the peace and freedom for which it was intended. The fallen existed to tempt the weak and to torture the strong. This, as it is written, is not to be. Before time there was space and before life there was a new way to be as God was, pure as the Temple, pure as the Light of man preserved. The Protectors of the Light promised to uphold the Light in all areas of the universe. They will always be part of the Temple "as it is and will always be."

Several hundred years from the time of destruction, there was a change in how God was seen by the Angels—a different way of being than when they were assigned. Different levels of Elohim or Angel Guardians were assigned to protect the child of God, Jesus, when he was resurrected from the grave. Decades of Angels were all worshipping the God child, Jesus, who left with them and created another reality of space and time, which was protected by the Brotherhood of Light. Until that time there had been only one congregation of Angels. It will be noted that throughout history man connected with Jesus as the son of God, but in fact, an alternate reality was created to distance from the son of Jehovah. Newer documents show that when this division took place, a small number of the congregation of Angels wished to join the newly anointed king and continue the pursuit of love and happiness in this other paradigm. Many modern day accounts of this chain of events prevent others from learning their own truth as it pertains to their mission on Earth.

Because of disagreement among all the accounts of how the world was started and fell, man has not been able to move beyond this reality. What we fear is still holding us back from what we know. Until that trust has been reestablished, we will be keepers of the truth as it pertains to Earth and those who inhabit it. General characteristics of this new-age chain of events keep the general population locked in the Jesus reality. There will always be truth within the soul of each child. The child knows his true form and will pursue this only when he feels free to do so. The current Earth environment has made this a difficult task as organized religion, with good intention, assumes that we are all of the same truth. Even before organized religion, the truth, as it was best known, was taught by other elders. This is human nature and evolution, but we must now break through the barrier of what we knew before and what we know may be.

Move to a place of acknowledging that there is more than we see with our eyes and formulate a new reality that requires us to include all that we have previously discarded because others did not believe as we did. Be the keepers and inventers of change. You can always be as you are, but when you push that aside, it allows for your formidable truth to emerge. The challenge at hand is to create a trust in God and all that God stands for in the evolution of this planet. Division is not the answer. Small changes yield large results in all men. Move forward with the mission as it was created—without "original sin" as you call it. Believe that the answer lies within you and all that you claim to be.

Author's note: The most important point in this section is to let our children grow into their own with guidance but with room for their own development. Allow for them to make choices and bend the way we see things so that the bigger picture can emerge. Let religion assist instead of dividing people. Embrace the truth of others even when it is outside of our belief systems. It is only fear that keeps us from embracing the love of all religious faiths. We have to be the bringers of change, and our children are here to help with this process. You have to believe that there is something more than war and battle for power, and you have to want more for this world and our future.

Why Did God's Son Luciferis Leave Heaven?

When Heaven was created to sustain the Holy Spirit and the souls of man, Luciferis was assigned by God to watch over the gates. Luciferis became bored, 8,000 years after creation, with the task of watching the gates of God's Heaven. He wanted to create his own version of Heaven. Luciferis saw the intent of man was far below him and thought that the heavenly host should not be watching the children of God. He became jealous of the people and souls of Heaven and wanted them to call him God as he believed he was just as powerful. God warned Luciferis that he would disrupt the perfect balance of Heaven and of creation if he chose to create another place where he was called God.

God wanted to appease Luciferis with a sanctuary of his own called "The Garden." This angered Luciferis, since he would still be second in line to God. Luciferis wanted more than what God would allow him to have. The price of this was excommunication and placement in a Second Heaven, where he would have to spend eternity in solitude beneath God. Luciferis again betrayed God by stating that he would remain as God wished and return to his task of watching Heaven. God was overjoyed and welcomed Luciferis back to his post. When the Host of Man was unaware, Luciferis fell to Earth and vowed to destroy the efforts of his father. Man would be defiled by Luciferis' revenge against God.

Author's note: Before I could even hear this section, I had to put aside all that I had been taught while growing up. As a child in Sunday school, I had been told that Lucifer was a fallen Angel, which to me meant that he had originally been created by God at the level of an Angel. To open my mind to the prospect that co-creation was a possibility was very difficult. I asked what I needed to do to open my mind, and God had me draw three adjoining circles. The center circle was labeled God or Goddess. The adjoining circle to the left was labeled Holy Spirit and the adjoining circle to the right was labeled Luciferis. Underneath was the word co-creation. Every time my mind has heard something that has been outside of my mindset, it has been disturbing at first until I spoke to God about it. When I heard this, I needed to know that even though Luciferis existed at the beginning of creation, he was not as strong as God. It was explained to me that there is an imbalance because of Luciferis' fall and because he no longer maintains that place next to God in co-creation, so other areas of existence were having to make up the difference to maintain balance. It was also explained that co-creation is not a scary topic unless you dislike the accountability for stabilizing your world yourselves. Evil can only exist where our accountability has failed.

The Universal Truth

In the beginning there was a supreme truth that everything that was will always be. Now there are many truths that have replaced the previous versions of the same. In front of God we stand in our truth as it relates to "all that is," and in some cases the meaning of what we once were improved over time—a lift or ascension of who we are. The smallest truth is the one that is never told. God says to stand in your truth. Be the warrior you are now and will become. Become the warrior that you were striving to be today even though you may not have reached it on this playing field. Stretch your limits to include the outdated versions removed—a new you. Lift a finger to peace and control of the wicked. Balance your earthly desires with those of your spiritual truth and integrity.

Eons ago there was a supremacy theory that those who were outdated were killed. This is not a truth of God. This is a truth of the Devil, a new name given to Luciferis in this day and age. Supremacy is the truth of the Devil and not man. Do not take this plan of action, as it makes you negligent of God's plan. Negligence will cause nations to fall and killings to continue unnecessarily. In the year 2041 you will find a crossroads where you can no longer hold back the dam waters of your people. Many will be lost if you do not focus on the truth of God and love.

You are the keepers of the storm and must accept change to stop the growth of Satan, another name for Luciferis. Who are you to claim that there is good in all when you do not see it in yourself? Move the garden variety seekers aside and allow the true leaders to emerge and create the growth and change that is required. Don't hesitate to help your fellow man because that hesitation will cost lives. There is accountability for neglect and hesitation when you could have saved a life by owning who you are and making a difference.

Silence is not the answer to economic and spiritual power. The fall of man will be in lack of economic power if you do not change your ways. The people who control this part of the Earth are only focusing on the immediate power and the need to feel this power. Sometimes the answer is not in the power of people but the trust in people. No one trusts anyone in your world. Can you imagine what would happen if everyone started to trust and rely upon one another? True spiritual change would occur. When you make that connection with others, you will find the thing that brought you together in the first place: a Divine plan for change and transparency, to become one with the Creator, "all that is and all that will be."

Truth is not in the eye of the beholder but in the face of true connection. True intention is the way to start this change you crave. ***"I ask my power to create a better world to be unleashed—opening the very depths of my Soul to connect with others here to make a change in this world."*** Too many times we neglect the formidable truth as it allows others to see our true power. In a world of mistrust, this is almost impossible until a few brave souls come forward and grant the permission of many—opening the doors to what can and will be because we all have a common bond and a need to survive.

Author's note: The Tablet is written where space and time do not exist as we know them. This information was explained as the equivalent of God attaching a stick-on note to the Tablets.

Heaven's Gates

The reason that Heaven was created was to serve man and to provide refuge between life experiences, a holding place for the souls of man. Beneath Heaven was a Second Heaven. In 2034, actual worlds were lost to the fallen and required protection from the souls of man on Earth and other planetary homes. This place was protected by the Angels and will provide a standard connection to God and protection from the wicked. Heaven was originally a peaceful retreat center where souls could congregate to bring the conscious awareness of the existence of more than Earth and planetary life into the human experience and to sense the closeness to "all that is, was, and will be." Even in the beginning, the souls of man made mistakes and were evolving as human beings and as souls. This is why Luciferis was assigned to oversee this place of soul growth.

Angels are able to move through space and time without barriers in order to locate and neutralize the fallen and to bring lifetimes into alignment with God's word. Even with the assistance of God's word, this process is on-going to restore the universe to what it was in the beginning. The beginning is the time when "all that was and will be" was love.

Why God Added Man

Without man, the existence of God remains the same. God chose to acquire a new area of growth for his universe and introduced man. Man would start simple and pure and would be a reflection of God, which would extend out into the universe. Universal love is pure and does not need anything else. It is the pure connection of God and the Divine within "all that is." Many creations have inspired God, but not as much as man. Man was the beauty of innocence and love for eternity, without strife and chaos. The vibration of man could be felt across all plains of existence. God loved man and man loved God. Many lifetimes on Earth were pure love this way.

Original Sin and God's Response

Luciferis has brought much unnecessary pain and chaos to Earth. Man has adopted a program that comes from Luciferis, which states that all men are responsible for the first sin of man (the first time that they strayed from love and that existence). Luciferis says that man must endure pain for his brother. No one is immune and all should suffer a painful death and birth.

He, who has chosen not to run from Luciferis but to endure this unnecessary pain, will be given part of the Temple to place in the pocket of their soul until the time that they have chosen their truth over the anguish of Satan. Satan is not your truth and keeps you from experiencing the love of the Temple. Try to remember who you are and who you started to be before Satan locked you into his belief that all are punishable by him. Beliefs that are not yours make you yearn for what you need to be, but you cannot get there unless you have love break this bond. Hatred will only cause it to take hold further. Self-doubt will only make it stronger. Self-doubt is responsible for endless pain and torment. Luciferis counts on this as his best and most reliable way to keep you from your truth. He makes you doubt who you are.

When you know who you are, you will no longer be bound by this punishment and will be allowed to experience peace in who you are as a soul. When you visit Heaven, where the loving souls congregate, you feel this pure vibration of love. Often you will remember this experience in an effort to remind others of what "is and will always be"—the pureness of love as God and the entire universe know it. Expect that the days of Heaven will always be love. Picture your visits there and breathe in the essence of the Temple and God's love, and this will untie any unnecessary bond with the Devil.

Who is the Son of Jehovah?

Before there was Jesus, there was Enoch. Enoch is the character that you see when the end of the world comes, and he is the savior from unnecessary punishment. It is his belief that you will always be part of his army and will no longer need any other belief except his. He stops endless wars and moves civilization to higher degrees when you allow yourself to be a true creator of the Lord's truth. The truth he instills allows others to find their starting place in the universe and to conquer the demons ahead. He can't stop until the purpose for his existence is met with victory. This was not his plan, but God's plan for him. He loves God more than life and is dedicated to serving all that God has assigned him to do. He feels this is a large task for such a small man in comparison to what he believes he is: a child of God and a tiny speck in the vast creation of the universe. To the day of this writing, he still wonders why God has chosen him, just an ordinary man, to take on the task of the world and the peace therein.

Sometimes he and God spend countless hours considering how to grow man to a new level, a new reality, a different way of handling the same neglectful situation in which men war and kill on a continual basis. Enoch does not want to hurt man but, instead, wants to love the soul part of each until the end of time. He does not know that he will always be the fighter for change. He is often hidden away as an ordinary man, but he sometimes gets a lifetime of glory. He does not ask for much, except a chance to serve because he loves God so much. He places his love in God's hands and allows the creation of new and grander things to emerge. Sometimes he loses faith, but each time he grows stronger and his bond with God is unparalleled.

Enoch demanded that the outcome of the universe should be up to God, not man. God often explained to Enoch that change, as small as it may be, will bring about large-scale growth if given time. If left alone, a small change will move to other changes, which bring the Earth to a place of contentment—the first step of love. If we can believe in change everlasting, then a small change means more. God told Enoch that he was not going to force the change and was going to let it happen in its own time. Unfortunately, Enoch was going to have to be patient and work with God, even when he did not agree.

Seven Ways to Overpower Satan

1. Drink from the Fountain of Knowledge. Inside the Seventh Heaven is a small lake filled with knowledge and God's plan for all of his children. Go to this place and free your soul from pain and anguish. Move into the Light that makes you pure, the way God intended for you to be. Bring your children and their children until all are pure and free.
2. In the Seventh Heaven all things impure are made pure. Enter with disease and leave clean. The tortured souls are not left to die. They will be brought to the level of existence where they should have been—impurities lifted and souls complete. When Satan takes the souls of children, there will be a price paid by him, not God's children. If you are a son of God, you are protected by the Light of God, and his team of Angels is here to protect you and your children. This is as it "is and will always be," in God's name.

3. Ask for grace to be bestowed upon you. Satan is powerless against God's name. God sends you out into life with his grace and the wings of his Angels wrapped around you. The smallest whisper for God will bring this to you.
4. God has a breed of "Punishers of Satan" called Do-Se-Ta /doe-say-tah/. They restore joy to souls who have been taken by the wicked, and they restore grace to all of God's children. To regain peace when there is soul possession by the wicked, call for Do-Se-Ta.
5. Visit God's Temple Sakura, which is located 108 degrees south of Mt. Vishnu. That is where the soul connection can be made that connects you to your destiny as written in the Journal of Records and contained within your soul contract with God and Earth. When you have forgotten this in Earth life, allow yourself to axis this connection [go to your higher Light] in meditation. a) Breathe two breaths of peace. b) Breath two breaths of hope. c) Say one prayer to God. d) Release sin. e) Enter the Temple. This is when you will see who you are. No one can keep you from your own records.
6. Ask Satan what his business with you. He has to tell the truth. Lead him to Creator, as God is your savior not him. Pray for his soul and leave.
7. The center of Lemuria is located within the eastern center of Russia near the Temple of Men. This was once the center of all life on Earth before the demise. Place a hand over your head and pray for peace. Hold your overlapping hands on your heart center until you reach your connection to "all that is and will be." Immediate relief will be found.

Stopping the Spread of Evil

There will always be evil that circles the Earth until man stops viewing God as a supreme being who creates and controls all things. God is the main source of energy in your world, universe, solar system, and beyond. The fact that you view God to be one individual opens the universe to the thought of opposition. God is the central gathering place of peace and love, the unity of the universal Light, and the freedom from chaos. This source fuels the continuation of "all that is"—not one being, male or female, but the energy of creation. The mere thought of physical form is started at Source energy or God. Creation is vastly co-creative after that. God, Goddess, Source, Buddha, Allah, Jesus, and so on are all versions of the same purest form energy at Point Zero. Please don't rule out the purest form just because it does not reflect your current belief system.

All of you are responsible for the co-creation of the planet Earth in the next phase of existence. This existence of all does not solely depend upon God. God is the energy you connect to when locating Point Zero, and you bring that energy into you and all that you do. This is how change happens. When we co-create with God, we connect with the highest, purest form of creation and send this throughout. Connecting with the highest, purest form of creation is not being judgmental or condemning of others. It is not warring over religion or the possessions of others. That comes not from a place of pureness, but a place of evil. Call this evil or whatever you like, but it is in opposition to the highest, purest form of creation. You will lose this place you call Earth if you continue the process of creation together with the opposition to the highest, purest form of creation.

The truest form of beauty is when the lost are brought to Point Zero creation. This is the renewal of faith, love, and trust in the universal code of love and acceptance. Without this, nothing exists beyond your current paradigm. Universal doorways cannot be accessed without the Universal Code of Existence. Each doorway you open moves your world to new avenues of faith and justice. Justice is when the universal codes are upheld in a space of contentment with "all that is." Trials in your existence have brought you recognition of the wrongs in your world. The Universal Code requires you to connect to the highest, purest form of creation and to mend the ways of the wicked. Your table is not as it should be with "all that is." Lifting one side up and leaving the other unattended brings imbalance to the universal energy. All shall be created and lifted to the Point Zero creation. This is when balance is truly achieved—when all is lifted up. It is not just you raising your part, but when all points are lifted to this purest form of creation. Sickness is a side effect of imbalance in the Universal Code of Existence. This does affect the physical part of your world.

For centuries your planet has studied how to reach the higher universal energy, but the lower place in your mind that activates your fears, inadequacies, karma, and death often reroutes you to a non-beneficial source. Make a decision to be a conscious co-creator of your universal, purest form creation by not allowing that part of your human mind to sink into self-limiting behaviors and belief systems created by this and others' ideas of power, sacrifice, and indignity. This is not working, and you are not accessing the higher part of your electrical connection to Divine Creator energy when in the lower part of your mind. You cannot be in the same place at the same time when it comes to your "electrical" connection with Source/Creator/Point Zero energy. You must choose the higher connection or the lower mind point. This is a choice as a conscious creator that you need to make. Do not blame others or your experiences for the lower connection, as this serves no purpose and promotes a more fear-based society, when you have no basis for this. Bring yourself to a place of enlightenment and agree to promote this energy in your world to lift the spirits of many and not just your own. The Universal Code expects you to bring each other upward.

Author's note: Writing this section caused some stirring of emotions for me. When I was able to move beyond the new wording, it was explained that we really just need to picture the center circle (the beginning point of all creation), plug ourselves in, and then bring that connection to the highest place God /Creator into all that we do.

Free Will

From the beginning of creation, a place was established in the universe to protect Free Will and the destiny of the planet Earth. Earth is a place of learning and a powerful place of truth. This truth is achieved by allowing each man a place to experience contentment and to build, to varying degrees, a multi-functioning grace, which is only achievable within the human experience.

Free Will creates this dimension of existence. It creates programs of change and diminishes the self-fulfilling prophecies before it. Growth of what you recognize as expressions of pure unconditional love create a new truth and level of being never before seen, felt, heard or experienced. Picture a flower suddenly becoming an intensely creative, self-functioning being of Light, a creator of peace and joy, and an elevation of the truth that started as a mere flower. Free Will is a way to bring universes and people together to contribute to a multi-faceted energetic process, which expands beyond the universe.

Sometimes you fall gracefully before you see another way—a way that works for all beings, not just a small group—a way for all beings to simultaneously create a higher level for all. Instead of a race to achieve individual happiness, it is a way for "all that is and will ever be." The layers and deepness of the Creator within "all that is and will always be," co-creating a new masterpiece of life. This is the way it is intended to be, not an illusion of anger and hatred that grows. It is a process of ever-growing, ever-achieving grace, which knows no limits of self-expression—an explosion of glorious waves of light and Point Zero creation mending and growing "all that is" with every connection it touches. See the universes as they are: endless continuing current of Creator in all of you.

Part II -
A Lightworker's Guide to Energetic Healing

The next segment of this book will be the author's experiences from her work, as a human Angel, to bring peace and discovery to those in the physical realm. She opens our minds and spirits to remember who we are and why we are here. Much of the Tablet information that has been shared is about how to open our minds to the larger energy we call God/Source and how to change the dynamic of fear/loss to love/acceptance of Divine Holy Spirit, which opens doors to our soul connection with God.

Part of being aware of "what is" requires examination of the ways energy and loss encourage the existence of evil/greed and discovery of how to overpower the evil that is still apparent in this current space-time continuum. Inaction results in the negative outcomes of this existence. When you choose not to acknowledge the problem and your part in it, you at the same time decide to accept society's ways of evil and ignorance to it. Who are the Lightworkers that came to the planet to make changes? Are some of them falling victim to the same energy that they came here to change? Create a space where your children and grandchildren can live in peace with one another. Choose action.

My Cup Overflows

I have spent some time speaking with God. This isn't something I had expected to happen. I lost a dear friend suddenly, and it just happened in my own way and in my own time. It defines the way I now think about life, before and then after. I had always been very aware that there was something more...something more than myself, my things, my job, and my income. But what happens when you are suddenly aware of deceased people around you? What happens to the reality that you lived and believed in, when your whole life changes? I realized that I needed to write about my experiences in connecting with more and connecting with God. This has not been an easy process. It takes determination as each step requires you to stretch your current belief system to an uncomfortable level over and over again.

I had gone to church a few times as a child, but not consistently. My beliefs were Christian-based, although I had a parent who also believed in reincarnation. Surely a person who attends church on a regular basis would be more entitled to this conversation than I. Right? Well no, I was told. Sometimes it takes a person who truly loves someone and loses them, to start a conversation with God in the first place. Why did she have to leave? Did I do something wrong? Did she do something wrong? Did she decide to take the cancer from her sister and leave this plane in her place? I got a "yes" response for that last question. She decided to "take one for the team" and left in her sister's place. Her sister has been cancer free ever since. That is a miracle to me. If I had never lost my dear friend, the conversation might never have started. She gave me a gift in leaving, just like she did for her sister.

Over the past few years, I have become very close with God, also called "Creator," "Source," "Universe," and many other names by others. I am pretty sure that I have asked enough "whys" to keep Him busy, just like I did with my parents. I would like to share some of the conversations, which did not always turn out as I had expected. I believe the dialogue will shock some and entertain others. It always does. Some will want to work on their own connection, and that is the main reason I wanted to share. I still don't attend a traditional church, but every day God is part of my life and the others I touch. Take what works and resonates with you and let the rest go. You will have to find your own right answer or truth. I just bring another perspective.

A Flower Unfolding

I sat down one day and asked God, "What makes you sad?"

The response was "...anger and hatred. The reason for your existence is based upon love and love only. So many shades of anger—so many lives are lost due to hatred. If you were to hold the most precious thing you own in your hand and watch it be destroyed before your own eyes, next to your own heart, you too would be sad. You tear the wings off the butterfly and expect it to fly."

My response was, "Why do you allow us to have Free Will, then? I don't think we can handle Free Will."

And God answered, "I am pleased with the changes that are being made to correct it. A life corrected turns into gold, and that gold is shared with all of existence. I believe in the strength of forgiveness. For centuries 'God' has been misrepresented by those who use God as a weapon, when there was no truth to statements used to create chaos. My words are not those of chaos, but peace.

Ask yourself, how much more loss will it take to cancel hatred? How many will succumb to an existence of sadness and anger? Will the heart break before it can be touched by God?

Anger is deeply crying to be released by your bodies, and painful illness resides when it is not released. Hatred is in the same place that you receive and feel God's love. If you are filled with hatred, God cannot speak to you as a soul. God will always love you as a soul, as His child, but you must open the space of hatred and transform it to inner peace. Do you want to feel what is your birthright? Then, this is what you must do. Release the hatred and anger that you are holding in that space. Say, '*God release me from this inner pain and torment; replace it with your love and abundance.*'

Make a decision to live in the peace and acceptance that not everything is a reflection of your own being. You cannot change what has been done to you, but you can accept serenity. Cancel any sadness that is not yours. Cancel any fears that are not needed. Cry if you need to and be free. Peace is a place located deep within your soul. Go to this place when you breathe, when you grieve, and when you are seeking a deeper connection to that love you are as a soul."

Even Though I Walk Through the Darkest Valley, I Fear No Evil
(Psalm 23:4, New International Version, 2011)

"You can't make change in the world if you won't speak your truth. Too many times, throughout history, tragedy could have been averted had someone spoken when they knew something was wrong. Many lives have been lost as a consequence of someone not speaking his or her truth. The soul that is willing to take a chance will make change; the soul that does not will feel defeat. This is not a consequence of God, but of you. Those who know someone who is capable of inflicting harm, but they do or say nothing, will feel defeat if this inaction results in the injury or death of someone else. This was not for God to handle, but for you. Why do you not speak your truth? What are you afraid will happen if you do? Is that fear real? Is evil real? Yes, evil is real.

Evil is the place where Ego meets negligence. You can't explain why you didn't help; you decided not to. Responsibility for deciding not to act when you could have is negligence. We watch in horror with everyone else, when we had the means to change it. What fear is so strong to cause this? You are afraid of being judged by your peers. What if the peers don't agree? Is that more important than taking a step to create real change? It seems to be, or you would act—even with the fear of being alone in your actions. You ask me why evil exists, when you perpetuate it with inaction. You ask, 'Why, God, do you let me suffer so?' and I say because you perpetuate inaction.

Inaction is the cause for all suffering. If you want change, you make it. What you are doing is not working. Try something else. Negligence is not going to change the suffering. Expecting someone else to carry your load is not working either. Take accountability for what you have created and change it. Ask for ways to make your world a better place, rather than to blame God for the injustices that you allow."

He Leads Me in Right Paths
(Psalm 23:3, The New Revised Standard Version, 1989)

Not everything you read in the Bible is accurate. Before Christ, God existed. Consider that what you have been told may be just a chapter in a larger book. Where are your chapters for before Christ? They are in your soul. Who you are cannot be rewritten or changed to suit others. Each individual suspects that there is more than what is written in the Bible, but they are judged for exploring their inner consciousness because this does not fit with the teachings of their church. Why did you ever think that God was a bully? This is the greatest misuse of "church" because a church is a place of worship, not control. Why are we afraid to learn who we really are?

It is apparent that you believe in more; you reach new levels of knowing with each progression in technology and medical advancements. This would not be possible if you were to stay strictly within the parameters of the Bible. Each time you substitute one belief system for another, you reach another level of consciousness. The old is no longer written in stone, and you break out of the barriers of your minds. You create freedom to grow and develop those areas that are no longer working. As long as you are open to new possibilities, this growth will never cease. If I were to tell you that Jesus never walked the Earth, you might become stubborn in your Ego. What is wrong with seeing if a new way of looking at things resonates with you? What if I were to tell you that God is a mathematical equation? Can you prove that Jesus walked the Earth? Can you prove that the Bible was written as God's word? God is not a mathematical equation, and Jesus did walk the Earth—just not for the reasons you provide. Following a path of spiritual evolvement does not mean hurting another based upon religious beliefs. God comes in many forms by many means, so judgment is not necessary.

December 21, 2012

On October 11, 2012, I noticed a strange movement of souls. I could see them gathering on almost every street and rooftop. They were all waiting for something, like they were lining up for a parade. I asked Source what was going on in the spirit world. It was explained that a large number of souls who had been incarnating here on Earth were being transferred to another place. There were so many that it was going to take until December 21, 2012, for them to move to another planet-like, spacecraft location.

This is what the Mayans saw as the mass exiting of the planet. Most of these souls were already deceased and in their soul body and had consented to moving with the group. I would watch them cross the street and disappear into another place. Many people that I connect with felt the change in energy, but no one else saw the streets lined with souls. I, of course, had questions about why this needed to happen and was told that all souls would be relocated to other places before the Earth was no longer lit by the sun. Source also said that the next time this many souls were scheduled to leave would be in 1,000 years. The sun will no longer light the Earth on December 21 in 209,399 years. Everyone will be moved well before then.

Alignment Perceived

Focusing on what is out of your personal alignment drains life force energy. This is not the energy you need to make change. This energy will keep you where you have always been. That same comfortable place you go to. All sides are evenly spaced in the way you like and are used to. Nothing smells bad and is perfect in the way you like things. That is a way to never change. Is this where you want to stay? Is this the place you have always dreamed of?

What if I told you that when you accept the current chaos in your life as being in alignment, you would then be able to reach into the creative place in your mind that allows for new ideas and unlocks potential that you never knew existed deep within you? The energy needed to change your current picture of the world, your paradigm, starts with the acceptance that all is currently in alignment.

Who Are You Channeling?

How do you know that the person claiming to channel an Archangel or spirit guide is actually channeling what they say there are? You don't. To begin with, there are many different aspects of our own selves and soul self. We have an Inner Child and an Ego from this lifetime. We have a Subconscious and a Soul Body. The Soul Body has connections to our Higher Self, which is a compilation of all the experiences we have had in a body or between lifetimes, and more. We can channel all these aspects of ourselves. A person may have Soul Fragment, a part of themselves lost during a traumatic lifetime experience such as a sudden loss or death. Your Inner Child may be terrified to allow you to go forward because it still needs you to look at something from this lifetime that you have not wanted to look at. What if you are an Archangel grounding that energy here for this lifetime? Archangels also have an Inner Child, Ego, and Subconscious. They can have attachments at the soul level. So are you channeling the Ego of the Archangel, or the attachment that may have caused them to fall from grace? Are you entitled to channel this energy, or is it not in your highest good and purpose? Have spirits taken advantage of our Ego's need to say that it is talking to Jesus? Absolutely. Any energy can be mimicked if you are not acting in your highest good.

I remember attending my first channeling. A woman claimed to be channeling the female counterparts of two Archangels. I remember feeling a demon in the background of what she was channeling. It made me feel fearful and uncomfortable, and at the time I did not understand why. Why should something meant to be helpful and uplifting make me feel this way? When it was my turn to ask a question of the entity the woman was channeling, I asked (prompted by Spirit, of course), "What is the difference between dark and evil?" The energy being channeled said, "You attract this to yourself." I could feel I was standing up to something that was not of God and Light. I was feeling sick to my stomach and extremely anxious, like I needed to leave. I did some breathing to keep myself centered, and I stayed. Being somewhat new to channeling at the time, I approached this woman on a later occasion and told her that I could remove the lower energy from her. She was very upset and made sure to allow everyone to know that I was forcing healing crystals on her. After a period of time, I learned more about what was happening, and I recognized that I could not have removed this from the woman because it was part of her. I had a lot to learn then, and I know that I still have a lot to learn now, even with the experience that I have at this time.

Our mind learns in layers. I learn all I think that I can learn about in one area, and then the universe unveils another layer. I do not expect the unveiling to stop. I am also aware that our physical minds cannot comprehend the complete reality. Time and space travel is not at all what we believe it to be. It is more a conglomerate of many levels of existence in a space-time continuum resulting from endless connections and Light. It is a space-time sandwich that exhausts the human mind's attempts to envision it. We learn what we are able to learn in a way that makes sense to us. Growth at the soul level is reminiscent of the way we believe Jesus exhausted his effort to help humanity. It makes the wide-ranging reach of the universe almost inconceivable to the human mind.

We can't change what is directly in front of us unless we can see it. Seeing requires you to move with energy and not to trap it. Why are Angels in the human realm? They want to help us to see what is right in front of us. Without an expansion of the space-time realm, we will never reach an understanding of what is hiding in plain sight. Cancer is a result of not seeing what is right there. It is a disease that breeds more of the same unless we learn to look at what is further than our physical form. We can't stop what we do not understand, and this is where we need to start. Allow the purest vibration of love to enter the place in your heart where your soul connects with the universe and beyond.

Reach Higher for Your Guidance

When you limit yourself to just your own higher knowledge, you won't benefit from the infinite supply of wisdom and Light at the Creator level. To connect higher than your own level, move your connection from your Higher Self to Creator level. This allows you to grow at the speed this lifetime offers.

If you receive guidance from God/Creator/Source level, you will receive the highest level of guidance for your current path. If I have nineteen guides and ask a question, I will generally receive nineteen slightly different answers. At a certain point, I realized that I should only get information from the highest source possible. I do appreciate all the love and support from my Angels and guides, but I still need the highest answers that pertain to this lifetime. We tend to outgrow our Higher Selves and have to make sure that the connection we are aligned with is at God/Source level only. This will keep you on your path and will help you navigate the unknown with God.

Some of you are here grounding the energy of your Higher Selves, which can be Ascended Masters, Archangels, the Holy Spirit, and so on. In this case, you will see that once you have healed your Inner Child and Ego on this plane you will encounter your Higher Self's Inner Child and Ego. You become a healer for your Higher Self. At times, the Ego of a Higher Self is difficult to deal with because it is very set in its ways. Do not assume your Higher Self knows more than you do.

Much physical illness is a result of the soul finding ways

to teach itself. This lower part of the "Inner Child" at the soul level believes it knows better than God and that it knows the best experience for its own needs. It comes from a place of fear within the soul due to experiences the soul has seen on many levels beyond the physical Earth life. These experiences cause us to misjudge reality based on circumstances that do not apply to human life. The soul is strong, and when the lower Ego/Inner Child part plugs into a fear-based human response, it is often locked into overwhelming discord. The key is to acknowledge the existence of more than we know, and let God sort this out for us.

Getting Your Signals

When working intuitively to use healing tools in energy work, it is essential to have a signal between you and your higher guidance. The signals can be unique to each person, and they are communicated through a body signal or other method. A signal may be a tone in one of your ears, a physical sensation, a visual signal, or it may be a "knowing." The use of a pendulum (dowsing) is also a great tool to connect with your Divine guidance until you work to receive information through another method. Working with your guidance usually takes time, and you may have to work/ask to make your signals stronger or clearer. Following are a list of body signals that will help you to choose tools and to properly clear and heal areas in a person's energy field.

Do a 5 minute meditation followed by sitting quietly to get this information:
    First breathe in the Divine Light of God/Creator energy and allow any distractions to be moved away from you. Center yourself in a place of love and beauty. Allow yourself to be lifted

to a place of complete clarity and connection with "all that is." See yourself in a room with God/Creator energy, where nothing else is present but you and God. At that time, you will ask for signals to help you in your path.

> Yes_____
> No_____
> On Target_____
> Spirit/Entity present (not Divine guidance)_____
> Energy Blockage_____
> Healing needed_____
> False Statement or information_____
> Truth_____
> Clearing _____
> Danger_____
> Cancer or serious illness_____
> Difference between Divine guidance and imposter entity
> _____
> Animal guide_____
> Elementals (fairies, nature spirits, etc.)_____

These are areas to start with and work on daily during a 10 to 15 minute meditation. If nothing comes to you, don't worry. Keep trying. You tune yourself in and raise your vibration every time you sit quietly with God.

How Energies Get into the Energy Field

Can energy that does not belong to the person you are reading show up in the field of the person, thing, or situation you are reading? Yes it can, for various reasons. If a person is the caretaker of an individual, often that person will be part of the overall energy and aura of the person you are reading. Other situations involve areas of the person's field that are open to attachment by those in physical or non-physical body. These entities are draining and can represent a permanent corded bond: an ex-lover who can't let go; a spirit who can't let go of the Earth experience to transition to the next level; traumatic events (from past, present, and future lives) that have not been healed. A vortex, or opening, can allow for attachments by an unauthorized spirit or energy. These attachments are generally located in the emotional area of the aura on the left side of the person's solar plexus.

The aura has layers where different energy connections are made:

The PHYSICAL BODY is the physical layer.

The ETHERIC BODY is the energy gateway layer between the physical and non-physical, moving energy in both directions.

The EMOTIONAL BODY is where the current state of emotions including positive and "negative" emotional experiences are located. Holding "negative" or draining emotions or patterns in this area can lead to physical symptoms and illness. The flow of energy can move into the physical body or affect the outer auric bodies. Examples of draining emotional energy are hatred, anger, jealousy, fears, and worries. In healing work this is the area where "spirit attachments" are located.

The MENTAL BODY is where our thoughts and beliefs are located. If we live our lives sending out affirmations, prayers, and other positive thought forms, the different layers of our bodies will benefit. Doing the opposite will cause a negative or draining effect on the other layers.

The SPIRITUAL BODY in healing and clearing work is the layer that contains outdated vows and contracts, karmic and past life issues, and curses.

I have noticed that when energies enter a person's field

during a burst of anger, hate, jealousy, or similar emotions, the energies do not seem to attach immediately but can be felt or seen at that time. You can check to see if energies are present by dowsing with a pendulum or other tool or by using your own body signals to confirm. The areas that I have seen to be vulnerable are the crown, third eye, back of neck (throat chakra). Proper protection layers are important when doing this work. I like to use Young Living Egyptian Gold (Biblical oils) on these susceptible points. Another vulnerable area is the GB-24 acupuncture point, which I feel under my rib cage on the right side of my chest. I have found that Myrrh essential oil is effective on this point.

There are many types of spirits, entities, and energies that come here from other dimensions. They usually do not have the living person's best interest at heart and need to be removed from the auric field to allow the body not to be drained or to allow it to access the energy it needs to better heal itself. If we are to remove energies from a person's energy field, we have to know what action to take and how to properly do the work. It is so important to be able to work with your higher guidance, which comes from a different perspective and knows what needs to be accomplished and how to do so.

Mediumship and Healing

We tend to classify the energies that a medium deals with as those of Earthbound Spirits. I originally defined the Earthbound Spirit as one who had lived on Earth in a physical body, but who then was not willing or able to return to Source when the body died. They stayed here because of unfinished business, shock, guilt, shame, fear, or other reasons. I have learned that this is only partially accurate. I want to begin by giving my own definition of mediumship. To me this is very simple. A medium is able to sense energies with their own methods and translate that energy into messages and actions that can be understood.

When we discover an entity, we can try to discover why they are here and if they need to be returned to their place of origin. Many times healing on some level is necessary before they can return. It is not necessary to channel or speak their words in order to help or assist. We can use our intuition and intent to help them remember positive memories from when they were in physical form. This will bring love or happiness to mind, which will raise their vibration, enabling them to see or acknowledge the Light. We call in Angels and others to help with healing and insight on what the spirit needs in order to move on. When a spirit is not cooperative or unable to heal at that time, Archangel Michael will assist by taking them to a holding place to heal. Often the same spirit is brought back to the medium when they are ready to cross over.

If you feel drawn to interacting and assisting the spirits to cross, this is probably something you have agreed to do while you are here. Whenever you are sending healing, either in person or remotely, you will often be assisting the spirits without even knowing that you are. When sending healing to entities or spirits that need it, try different ways of healing. Reiki symbols and crystals are just as effective on the nonphysical. When using a pendulum for this work, there will be a counterclockwise swing and then a 12 and 6 swing to fill the area with positive energy and for realignment. Picture holding the pendulum over a clock face or print one out to use as a chart.

Common crystals for releasing the energy bond between the physical and the spirit attachment include: Black Tourmaline; Smokey Quartz; Fossils and Petrified Wood; Moldavite; Fulgurites–Lightning strikes in sand; Iron-Nickel meteorites; Larimar; Garnet; Selenite. If you find that you often intuitively place these crystals on the left hip area of the person you are healing, then you probably have identified an entity that needs a higher vibration to break the energetic bond. These attachments can be from this lifetime or others. Check with you higher guidance to see if it is a past life issue attachment, a 10-4 swing. If this is the case, the person will have to address the entity with love and release the bond with forgiveness.

> **Releasing Attachments Prayer:**
> *I choose to allow love to replace any unresolved energy from other lifetimes or places of existence, with other people or energy that is no longer in my highest good to hold. I ask God/Creator/Source to bless my path in all directions of time and space so that I may be free of anything keeping me from being free. And so it is.*

After a 10-4 swing for a past life issue, you might then get a 9-3 swing, which means that further information is coming in psychically to give a better idea of what happened in the past life. That information sometimes needs to be known by the person before it can be successfully cleared. In other situations, it does not seem to be necessary to know all of the details.

Use your pendulum or body signals to know when spirits are present. When these entities are removed, the area of the aura that is damaged should be filled with love and Light. Use energy healing and Divine guidance. Crystals can help to repair the aura. Examples of crystals to wear to help repair the aura are Faden Quartz, Rose Quartz, and Spirit Quartz.

I think the most valuable lesson that I have learned while working with Earthbound spirits is that they are exactly like us. They are us, just without a physical body. They are often hurt and need healing of some kind. I believe there are no "throw aways." Often a spirit who has hurt themselves or another has attachments of their own, which had a direct influence on decisions they made. When doing the work and releasing the spirits and entities, include all attachments as part of who you are healing, or ask the Angels to help remove them. Work on your connection with your highest guidance as this will be vital in knowing what to do in different and unique situations. There will always be something to learn in this work, so be open to that knowledge. I know that love and healing is central to all.

Intuitive Crystal Healing

Enjoy this journey with your own higher guidance. When you notice patterns during your healing sessions, keep notes for yourself—or compile them, as I am, to reach others. Look at crystal healing as a new adventure, and let it be a fun, investigative experience. Many of you have worked closely with crystals in past lifetimes and will start to remember as you do the work. It may seem natural to choose and place the crystals in a grid or body layout. Books give general guidelines for use of crystals, but you will see that there may be other uses specifically for the individual you are working with. You may find some unique combinations and uses that have not been published. Even if a crystal, intuitively placed, does not make sense to you, believe that higher guidance has communicated information to you outside your awareness.

Selecting and placing crystals can be done with the use of a pendulum until you are comfortable with your body signals. Your signal for choosing the appropriate stone and its placement can be verified with a pendulum; however, it is important not to limit your growth by depending too much on the pendulum. Work to fine tune your body signals for selecting and placing the crystals where they need to be. You may notice that you add new signals as you continue to work. I believe body signals are key to learning any healing modality with your higher guidance.

Be confident enough to put away the pendulum and just feel the energy. Before you begin a session, do a scan, with your hands, through the person's aura (energy field) to see what you perceive. When you feel or see something in the field, take a moment to identify what it is based upon where it is located in the emotional, mental, or spiritual bodies. The more you work with people, the more you will be learning and working with your higher guidance. Every day is a learning experience for me. My higher guidance assures me that I will learn every day until I return to Source. I find this very exciting. Rather than feeling frustrated, as I sometimes did when I didn't have ways to identify the energies, I now look forward to new, unknown energies.

Before doing a session, organize your crystals by color and/or chakra or just randomly based on your intuitive feeling/knowing. I group them by chakra and also by specific uses. I also keep Clear Quartz in a separate container for use when "flowering" around a group of crystals on a chakra to assist with opening. Each crystal resonates by color but also by energy. When I started working, I was surprised when a high vibration crystal like Phenacite would be indicated for use on a chakra other then the third eye. This was the energy a clogged or sluggish chakra needed to clear dense energies. When people have certain illnesses, you will see that the normal energetic chakra balancing will be different. Also, be open that the chakra layout may be different for those from other planets or dimensions, whose energies are unfamiliar to us. You will start to see patterns, such as with people going through similar life experiences, which will allow you another means of reading the energy once you place the crystals.

I acquired the types and quantities of crystals that my guides recommended. If you can't afford certain rare or expensive crystals or you don't have what you need, you can program **Clear Quartz** to hold that energy. **To program a crystal, hold**

it to your heart chakra and allow the energy of the intended crystal to come from your higher guidance, through your crown, and into your heart chakra, where it enters the crystal until you get your signal that it is complete. You can ask for the intended program to charge a crystal or ask to receive something better. You can dowse with a pendulum to verify for yourself that the programming has occurred.

Make sure that the energy is cleared from your crystals before you start working with them. Since energy practitioners often see one client after another, it is necessary to clear the crystals between sessions. Traditional clearing methods such as saltwater baths [only for those crystals that will not be damaged by this], contact with clearing crystals such as Selenite, moonlight, etc. are too time-consuming to be practical in this situation. **You can use your pendulum with your intent to clear the non-beneficial energies from the crystals. The pendulum will swing counter clockwise when removing and will swing clockwise to energize them. Use your intent for Divine Light to cleanse them, if you choose. Picture a golden white Light coming down from the Divine, bathing the crystals, and removing all dense and non-beneficial energies.**

When beginning a session with someone, always align yourself with the highest energies. Use your own method for connection. I use prayer and connect myself to my highest level guidance that is appropriate for the person. I place a "safety grid" around the individual to keep all non-beneficial energies contained away from the healing space. You can mentally picture this, or do as I do and, with this intent, place a physical merkaba above the crown chakra and below the earth chakra.

Be careful not to make the mistake of taking on the energy and emotions of those you work on. This is not your energy to take. I have worked on people with whom I have an emotional tie, and I could feel when I assumed their emotional baggage. It felt like a heavy energy being thrown and hitting my heart chakra. When this happens, the other person says that they are feeling better, and you are left with clearing work to do for yourself. When placing the grid around the person, include the thought and intention that you will do what you can for the person, and that you will not take on any non-beneficial energies, including those related to sickness, when working on them. Once a person is gridded and you are aligned, you start choosing crystals.

Raising the Vibration of Crystals

My personal vibration eventually raised to a level where a crystal such as Selenite became a grounding stone for me, and I could produce higher vibrations than the stones. I thought that I would no longer be able to use crystals for intuitive layouts and clearing work. Recently, I learned that there were higher "octaves" of the crystals' vibrations, and that I could have their vibration raised. This not only made them useful once again for me, but it also gave them a higher purpose and healing ability. When I discovered this, I was eager to explore new possibilities with various crystals. I felt a twinge of regret that I had already given away many of my stones, but I knew that I'd given each of them to clients and friends who had a need or use for their energy. I always trust that God will provide a way for me to have what I need when I need it, so I don't hold attachment. In actuality, the energy exists outside of the physical and can be experienced and utilized by anyone who is open to that reality.

The first stone whose vibration I raised was my faceted Kunzite pendant. This allowed me to open to higher states of subconscious and conscious connections as well as anything higher that was connected to love and Divine inspiration. When I asked how to raise the vibration of the stone, **I was told that my vibration or the vibration of others would raise the** stone's vibration. You can ask God/Source energy to raise the vibration for you. To observe this as it happens, hold a pendulum over the crystal and ask for the intention to raise the frequency of the crystal. The pendulum should first spin counterclockwise, then forward and back in a 12-6 swing, and then move as if outlining the petals of a daisy, before it stops.

I have made a list of applications for some crystals raised to their higher vibrations. There will always be additional higher vibrations and different ways to use them. Be open to your intuition. Keep that sense of play and learning by making time to go to crystal shops or rock shows and trying new stones and combinations. Most of what I have learned has been when there wasn't pressure and it was fun to work with my Source connection to invent new tools and ideas. I bring the Source connection into everything, including play.

Applications for Crystals Raised to Higher Vibration

Please take personal responsibility for your health and well-being, as well that of those you care about. This intuitive information is intended to guide you in clearing and balancing energies. It is not to be used as an alternative to seeking qualified doctors or professionals for medical or mental health issues.

Aegirine – The energy of this crystal begins in the solar plexus and then connects to the throat chakra. Creative voice. Aligns the Ego into the higher energies. Repatterning for old behaviors. It is also protective and filters negative energies from the field. Use to cut energetic cords contributing to physical illness. I used to use Stibnite for this purpose before finding the raised vibration of Aegirine to be more effective.

Alexandrite – This crystal brings golden healing Light down through the crown chakra, which cleanses and opens the chakras and meridians. At the same time, it connects with Mother Earth and brings its healing energy upward into the solar plexus. These two energies unite in the heart chakra.

Amber – Cleans and clears all chakras and meridian points. When there is illness such as that related to cancer and associated with lymph nodes, intestines, thyroid and other organs; Amber helps to remove energy stuck at both the physical and emotional levels. The crystal should be cleared every 5 minutes during body layouts to remove the dense energies it has collected. Combine with Rhodizite, as it will vibrate the disharmonious energy to the surface for collection by the Amber. Rhodizite should also be cleared in the same manner. The combination of Rhodizite and Amber distances fallen Angels and lower energies from your healing practice.

Amethyst – Assists with deep-rooted emotional hurt. The energy is directed down through the crown and into the heart chakra and solar plexus, where it goes deep to heal both the individual and the Inner Child. Aligns with the higher heart and oneness. Archangel Metatron energies.

Angelite – Opens the heart to higher vibrations from the Divine and enhances channeling and delivering Divine messages. The energy is very soft and supportive for the throat, third eye, and crown chakras.

Apatite (blue) – Helps with the energy of nausea, clears negativity from the lower chakras, and allows one to speak from their heart more than their Ego.

Apophyllite (clear) – Boosts the energetic system of those with cancer, which originates in the solar plexus. Raises the vibration in all of the chakras starting at the solar plexus. Combine with Selenite and Rhodizite. It raises one's vibration during meditation and allows for higher awareness during spiritual work.

Aquamarine – Clears the throat chakra for delivery of spiritual messages from the Divine. Higher heart and throat chakra crystal. Helps with fears of opening up too quickly to psychic information and gifts. Use with energy contributing to digestive disorders.

Aragonite – Clears blocks in the throat and solar plexus relating to unresolved Inner Child issues. Encourages one to speak one's truth.

Axinite – Repels negative entities and removes the energetic cords from negativity. Supportive for those experiencing lower back pain and nerve injuries.

Azurite – Aids psychic abilities/third eye and throat chakra. Strong third eye crystal. Place on the heart chakra, in body layouts, to align the heart with the throat and third eye.

Barite – Use to even out energy held within related to high blood pressure and panic attacks. Place on the throat chakra and solar plexus in body layouts. Helps to bring to the surface a way to acknowledge who you are without the fear of losing who you currently believe you are. A warm, healing energy filled with loving vibrations. I use the barite from the Linwood Mine in Iowa for this purpose, but use your intuition when choosing. Use to clear outdated vows and contracts in all directions of time. Opens channels for prosperity and abundance.

Bloodstone – Use for deep emotional hurts to the heart that affect the self-esteem or will. Place on the solar plexus to align the heart with the higher level vibrations of the Divine. Supportive energy when experiencing grief after the loss of a loved one.

Calcite – (clear, blue, orange)

Clear Calcite clears and raises the vibration in the third eye and higher chakras. It can be combined with Merkabite Calcite on the heart chakra, in body layouts, to assist with clearing the emotional origins of heart disease and other heart ailments. It will allow the treated person to identify the emotional patterns that are no longer serving them.

Blue Calcite assists in aligning the solar plexus with the throat chakra. Helpful for speaking the truth, channeling, working in groups without hesitation or fear.

Orange Calcite supports the sacral chakra where it connects to the heart chakra. Clears imbalances with the sacral/sexual when there has been sexual abuse (for both the victim and/or the offender). It can be combined with Clear Calcite on the throat heart chakra, in body layouts, to clear entities. This is also a good combination for a healing wand.

Carnelian – Connects the lower chakras to the higher chakras for a direct connection to the Divine. Enhances the vibrations to the third eye. High vibration crystal. Helpful in astral travel and deep meditation. Clears throat chakra blockages and energies related to lung or heart disease originating in the throat chakra. Combine with Phenacite for raising the vibration and transmuting denser energies from the field.

Cathedral Quartz – Assists in locating the root cause of a problem or fear. Brings you into Divine knowledge and to your own journal in the Hall of Records. Heightens psychic abilities (third eye and crown chakra, which are aligned with the heart chakra) and is useful in meditation. Connection to Ascended Masters and Archangels. Raises a person's vibration in all of the chakras in order to work with other Light beings. Fosters communication and cooperation in groups, raising the vibration of the purpose for which they were brought together. Connects us to Mother Earth and the Divine celestial beings. Helpful for interdimensional healing work.

Celestial Quartz – Connects the heart to the third eye and the crown. Flows like a shower of Divine white Light flowing into all the chakras after the connection to heart and crown chakra is made. Excellent for entity removal work and cleansing the aura.

Celestite – Clears debris on the third eye for better connection to spiritual information from the higher chakras. Use for public speaking and channeling when you want a clear message relayed.

Charoite – Use when the heart chakra and higher chakras are not connected. Combine with Selenite, Gold, Green Tourmaline and Lepidolite for removing past life and current lifetime blocks that are associated with the third eye and crown chakras. Combine these crystals to assist those who have autism, Alzheimer's, dementia and related conditions. This combination is also enhanced when Fossils are added.

Childrenite – Removes astral entities. Heals the heart chakra of anger issues specifically related to anger that is held in and not expressed verbally.

Chlorite Phantoms in crystals – Removes parasites, implants, and other higher dimensional debris. Clears blocks in meridians and chakras and helps the flow of "chi" in areas with blockages. Double terminated points can be placed between chakras on body layouts to run the energy from the Earth chakra and higher. Very useful in wands for detail work.

Chrysanthemum Stone – Grounds a person experiencing difficulty making transitions in life. We often find resistance when we are ready to move to a higher vibrational level. Helps ease the transition and helps to vibrationally transmute dense energy and patterns out of our energy field. Combine with Lepidolite to help with emotional heart issues during transition times.

Datolite – Connects us to the Earth and clears blockages in the heart to open psychic vision and a clear channel to Divine guidance. Useful when the energy of withheld anger has manifested as high cholesterol or heart problems.

Dioptase – Removes an entity when the attachment point was the heart chakra and/or jealousy created the vortex. Place on the GB24 acupuncture point and on the heart chakra for entity (or thought form) removal. To assist the energetic systems of those with breast cancer, place on the heart chakra and the Li13 point, on the left side.

Elestial Quartz – Opens to receive signals from the root chakra and the spiritual connection located in the solar plexus to transmute or heal outdated or dense energies. When you ground deeper into the Earth, there is another God/Source/Creator connection in the Earth. This energy is used to power larger healing for dense energies and quick clearing. You have to clear yourself of Inner Child and a deep-rooted fear before this connection is at an optimal level. Elestial Quartz serves as a repeater, sending out this higher energy to other realms and experiences through a strong, spiritual connection to achieve peace within each Soul Fragment that has been creating off-center vibrations for the person or place you are working on. Intuitively you will find many combinations using Elestial Quartz and other crystals to clear specific energies.

Epidote – Use for lifting jealousy and envy from people, places, or things. The attachment one has with energy that produces jealousy and envy is one of the strongest energies to clear. Holding this discontent often creates energies that manifest as cancer and illnesses of the reproductive organs or throat. When a person is ready to release this discontent, you can combine Epidot with Prehnite and place it on the back of the heart chakra. Allow the energy to release the hold and then use Barite to move the displaced energy away from the individual's field. Barite and Epidote make an excellent healing wand to remove stubborn emotional energy from the field.

Try Epidote and Prehnite together in a cage or a pendant to

work as a lie detector device. While wearing this combination, I experienced a coughing attack when I was told a high-level lie. My husband held the crystals and experienced another individual being truthful in a situation where they normally were not. I would love to be told about your experience with this combination.

Fulgurite – Place on both feet, in body layouts, to assist with circulation problems and diabetes. You can combine Fulgurite and Barite to energize the meridian system.

Galena – Use for energy related to any major illnesses that originated in the solar plexus and are connected to the heart chakra, which includes some cancers. Use with Lepidolite and Rhodizite to keep rooms clear of astral entities.

Hematite – Makes being around dense energy more tolerable when doing healing work. Hematite can extract energies related to cancer from the lowest and highest places on the energetic body. Cancels and deletes old patterns of abuse and creates a new energetic gateway for dealing with things on a higher level. Energizes the spiritual connection during times of stress or detoxification.

Kunzite – Allows in the natural gifts that you have earned over lifetimes of service to God/Creator energy. Opens the heart chakra to the Divine acceptance of who you are as a soul and why you have come to Earth. Aligns all chakras to higher heart energy and opens the Divine gateway to peace. The higher heart energy will keep you focused on the mission instead of on the obstacles. Focus and alignment with God.

Labradorite – Makes you more comfortable with looking at you mission or spiritual destiny without judgment or fear. Can be worn for this purpose. Use it as a wand to clear astral entities and Earthbound Spirits caught between lifetimes.

Larimar – Deep cleanses energy of the solar plexus and

heart chakra. Combine with Fulgurite and Limonite to alleviate fears of the unknown, limiting beliefs, looping, or any other patterns that are holding you back.

Limonite – Lowers your fear threshold. Hold the limonite, ground and center, take three breaths into the dantian [your power, located just under the belly button], lower your instinct, free you energy, release your fear, believe it worked, fill with unconditional love, and test by thinking about the fear. Repeat several times, if needed. If you can't completely remove the fear, it may be there either because of an experience you wanted in this lifetime, to protect you, or it is not time to release it yet.

Prehnite – Removes deep emotional ideals that are held within the thought patterns of the subconscious memory, which connects to more than the current lifetime. This memory is often false and limits the way you can grow and love when you reach higher levels.

Rhodizite – Moves and lifts energy at interdimensional levels in order to access or heal areas of the electrical meridian system of the universe, including personal healing. It raises the vibration of all stones, but that is not its sole purpose. You are missing the higher vibrational octaves of Rhodizite if you limit your mind. The dodecahedron is far-reaching. Hold it on blocked meridian or pain points to psychically receive information about what is held there. I have achieved the results of acupuncture without needles by using nontoxic, removable glue dots to attach the smaller, more powerful pieces of Rhodizite. Many more uses, yet to be identified, exist for Rhodizite raised to higher vibration.

Selenite – Powerfully cleanses the area around the spiritual destiny and solar plexus, God/Creator/Source connection. Place it under your healing table at this higher frequency.

Crystal Removal Tools for Energetic Parasites and Other Debris

Stones are attached to a Selenite wand base.

Removal end – Septarian

Follow-up end – Chalcopyrite. (Intuitively place fingers on the connections as you are working.)

Stibnite wands can also be used to remove energetic parasites and other debris.

Pendulum Healing—A Multi-Purpose Method for Reading Energy

> **Releasing Attachments Prayer:**
> *I choose to allow love to replace any unresolved energy from other lifetimes or places of existence, with other people or energy that is no longer in my highest good to hold. I ask God/Creator/Source to bless my path in all directions of time and space so that I may be free of anything keeping me from being free. And so it is.*

Another method that can be used for removal is a pendulum. Dowse to see if there are energetic parasites, and then ask for Divine help to remove them. Let the pendulum swing (usually counterclockwise) until all are removed from all levels of your being. This method can take as much as ten times longer than using a crystal removal wand. Working with more than one person can also decrease the amount of time needed for removal.

I originally learned to program a pendulum to get yes/no answers. After receiving Reiki attunements, I decided to practice sending healing energy remotely while holding my pendulum. I noticed all kinds of interesting combinations of swings that did not mean anything to me at the time, other than I knew that they were connected to healing and sacred geometry. If I was feeling strong dense energy, I would see the pendulum rotating in a counterclockwise direction and then a clockwise direction after that. I could feel/see that the dense energy was removed and positive filled the space.

I have always been very determined, and getting the information needed to help others has been a priority and focus of mine. My close friend Pat and I spent hours on the phone using pendulums to do healing work. Both of our gifts were developing during this process. We were discovering what each swing indicated and became excited when new ones appeared. While working together to clear the same situation, it was interesting to notice that each of our pendulums were not always doing the same swings, which demonstrated that we were sometimes working energetically in different ways on the same issue. I also noticed that we were not interfering with a clear reading of what our energy was doing when using this pendulum healing method.

The pendulum is actually just a way of seeing what your energy [or, if you have the intent, other energy] is doing at any time. You don't even need to hold it for the entire time as many of you are already actively healing the Earth, each other, yourselves, and so on at all times. You can use this method to clear chakras; clear and energize crystals, food, water, or land;

lower fears; and about anything you else can think of. If I ask God to bless the food we are eating, I can watch my pendulum spin strongly clockwise and then align it to our energy system (meridians) to our highest good and potential. You may not feel the need to hold a pendulum to show that there is energy in prayer, but it is interesting to see it, in addition to believing/knowing or feeling it.

Counterclockwise – Removing energy
Clockwise – Adding positive energy

10-4 Swing – Past life
9-3 Swing – Bringing in information relevant to a past life
12-6 Swing – Realigning energy – A flip up at 12, updating your journal in the Hall of Records

I started to see a common swing of the pendulum when checking my dreams. The pendulum swung back and forth in the direction of 10 o'clock and 4 o'clock. At a certain point in my development, I was able to ask and hear my guides tell me that this 10-4 swing was for a past life, which is an unresolved lifetime in any direction of time, in a physical body or not. Read the *Releasing Attachments Prayer* to disconnect and heal this energy. At times just reading the prayer will not be enough to clear it because knowing the related details from that past life is necessary for your growth and progress in this lifetime. Meditate or pray for more information so that you can release anything that is no longer serving you. If using the pendulum while doing this, you might then get a 9-3 swing, which means that further information is coming in psychically to give a better idea of what happened in the past life. Many times after clearing a past life, there will be a follow-up realigning swing of 12-6, with a flip up on the 12. This shows the updating of your new status in the Hall of Records.

Dreams offer an opportunity to heal. The next time you have a dream and wake during the night, ask your higher guidance why you had the dream. Use your pendulum, body signals, or other intuitive method and ask if this is a past, present, future life. If it is, take this opportunity to clear it. The dreams may produce extreme emotions. Feel the emotions, acknowledge them, and then release them.

1-7 Swing – Fears/Phobias or Germs/Viruses

If you are working on clearing blocks or healing fears, you may see a 1-7 swing, indicating fears or phobias and sometimes germs or viruses. You can ask for these to be healed to your highest good or to use the information for whatever reason you needed to be made aware of it.

11-5 Outdated vow or contract – Read the *Releasing Attachments Prayer*
10-4 (Past life) followed by 11-5 (Outdated vow or contract) – Read the *Releasing Attachments Prayer*
9-3 Cutting of draining energetic cords; bringing in additional psychic information; opening a chakra

Another common swing, 11-5, indicates an outdated vow or contract. This can mean that a business partner, living arrangement, or something else in this physical lifetime is not working out.

If it is an outdated vow or contract from a past life, you will first get a 10-4 swing followed by an 11-5 swing. A past life vow or contract could be an oath to seek revenge, a belief system that you once held, a religious vow, a set of rules that you were bound by, or a different way of thinking that has followed you into this lifetime. It could even be a well-intentioned promise to always remain with someone. To heal this energy, say the *Releasing Attachments Prayer*.

Vows or contracts often reopen if you come into contact with a person in this lifetime who has the energy of a person from the past life. You might feel negatively about someone who you don't know well, or you might feel a strong connection to someone, almost like a long-lost love, when you don't have that type of interest in them. Notice interactions or acquaintances in your daily life that seem to be difficult and frustrate you beyond what seems logical for the circumstances. After clearing certain types of energy, you may have a 9-3 swing, which indicates cutting of energetic cords. (This swing can also mean bringing in information or opening chakras if you are holding the healing pendulum over a chakra.)

2-8 Non-beneficial entity

Lightworkers who are using a pendulum to observe what they are clearing may get a 2-8 swing, which is an energy that is draining and not beneficial to their energetic field or environment. If this happens, you can ask God/Creator/Source to clear the energy, or you can clear it using a method you are comfortable with. As this is carried out, the pendulum will display the removal or disconnecting of the energy with a counterclockwise swing and then various additional swings depending upon the circumstances.

1:12 - 7:37 Meridian overactive
11:57 - 5:37 Meridian underactive

Meridian overactive and **Meridian underactive** swings are also identified on the following clock face pendulum chart. You can balance your meridian points automatically with this method, or be informed of the status of the energy in a given acupuncture point or energy meridian. Many times energy is trapped in these points, causing an imbalance. Use your intuition to obtain further details about the imbalance.

When you reach other energetic and knowledge levels, there are additional swings, including an asterisk (repatterning swing) and one that swings counterclockwise, transitions into a vertical swing, and then continues spinning like a helicopter blade over the top of your hand [going to another axis]. These pendulum descriptions are meant as an additional tool or way to read and heal energy if this resonates with you.

Part II - A Lightworker's Guide to Energetic Healing

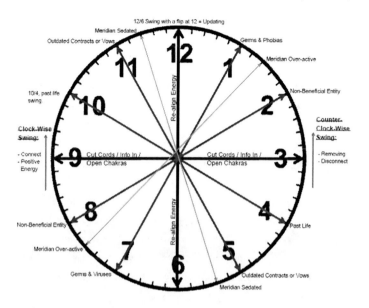

Swings of pendulum	Energy reading
Clockwise	Adding positive energy
Counterclockwise	Removing energy
12-6	Realigning energy / With a flip up at 12, means updating your Hall of Records
1-7	Fears/Phobias; Germs/Viruses
2-8	Non-beneficial entity
9-3	Bringing in information, often after 10-4; Cutting draining energetic cords
10-4	Past lives (Begin by reading the *Releasing Attachments Prayer*)
11-5	Outdated vow/contract (Begin by reading the *Releasing Attachments Prayer*)
1:12 - 7:37	Meridian overactive
11:57 - 5:37	Meridian underactive

My Experiences with Problematic Energies

One of my first interactions with demonic entities happened when I was working at a local metaphysical shop doing Reiki healing sessions for walk-in customers. I was a new Reiki Master/Teacher, and I knew that I needed to start working on more people, so I signed up. During some of my first sessions, items started to fall off shelves when I removed dense energy from people. The more I understood this energy, the more I realized that it was here to stop people from reaching their full potential by keeping them stuck in fear and old patterns of thinking. Many times this demonic energy was causing back pain on the left side as well as spasms. It was affecting spiritual workers of all types including energy workers, nurses, shamans, psychic mediums, among others.

The stronger the entity I was removing, the more I would hear its attempt to get me off-center with fearful thoughts. It was speaking in my ear, trying to gain any headway by targeting my issues that I was working on healing. Imagine removing a large entity while hearing that your children are in danger or that your husband is cheating on you. You keep your focus and follow through on what you are doing, saving anything that made you feel off-center to look at later. This experience made me aware of how important it is for energy practitioners to heal any vulnerable points that might be preyed upon by lower vibrations. Doing over 1,500 individual, group, and remote healing sessions since then has given me the opportunity to discover much more about demons, Fallen Angels, and other lower vibrational beings, and I have learned how to remove demonic entities without losing my center. I teach these methods to students and teachers of other metaphysical arts.

Demons are nothing more than low vibration beings whose goal is to cause chaos and fear. They associate themselves with hell and are a part of Satan's army. Once members of God's chosen team, Fallen Angels decided that they knew what was better for themselves than God and his plan for us. They chose to "fall" from grace, lingering with the other low vibrational beasts that choose to promote fear and despair. I have seen Fallen Angels return to Grace and know that this is possible when they are ready. I have also seen the cunning of a Fallen Angel using strategies to keep God's team here on Earth stuck in their own self-doubt and fear. I have never seen any of these beings be an actual cause for concern; however, I do see their energy as very limiting to spiritual and emotional growth. There are different versions of this energy in many dimensions and realities depending on one's belief systems.

It is rare that a person becomes possessed by a demon or low spirit, but it is possible. Many times a person's behavior, when they are in a weakened state of emotion or mental clarity, may be motivated by things the spirit is telling them to do. If the person suffers from mental illness or is high on drugs or other intoxicant, they may succumb to the influence of these low vibrational beings. I've found that remote removal is the ideal method for clearing attached demons or possession. I know that I do this work on the physical level and also on many other realms of existence, simultaneously. I know that I am protected by the Armor of God and the Light of Christ at all times.

I have, however, been energetically bitten, shoved, and pinched (but not harmed) by demons during removals. Recently I was experiencing nausea and pains to my physical body while doing my work. I needed to be made aware that it was possible for these low energies to cause pain, not only to the person having the demon removed, but also to the person conducting the removal. Either way, this tactic is used to make us stop the removal or to have the person we are working on become so uncomfortable that we stop the process. I have also had one of my dogs ram into me when I was removing an implanted program during a distance session. During this work, it is important to protect your home and animals, as well as yourself. Just place the Armor of God around yourself and everyone in your energetic area of responsibility and protect them with the Light of Christ. This will isolate them from any work that you are doing.

I have had people claim that I attract lower vibration energy to me or that I am looking for it. The reality is that what I do as a soul is clear this energy and other complicated spiritual attachments. I am grounding that energy here in this physical world. Because the lower energy would like us not to overpower it, it tries to make us second guess ourselves by any means that it can. It plays upon human strengths and weaknesses to cause division between our physical and spiritual soul selves. The minute you are out of your power, you are not as effective as you would otherwise be. Demons do not want us to figure out that they are powerless when we are in our power and connected to the highest vibration of ourselves. Fallen Angels do not want us to know that our Free Will and connection to God/Spirit outwits any game they decide to play. When you remember that you are a loving, powerful Light from God/Spirit, you begin to do the work you came here to do.

Psychic Children

It was a pretty slow "Free Healing Tuesday" at my office. Usually, on this day set aside for people to receive crystal, tuning fork, Reiki, and energy sessions by donation, there would be people waiting. When God told me to schedule these days, I trusted that the people who needed to would come. But here I was by myself cleaning, rearranging furniture, and wondering what He had in mind.

I was not getting any information. There had been a time when I was being given energetic previews of my day up to a week ahead of time. This was problematic after a while because I started to be anxious about what I was going to have to do to help people with uncomfortable issues like demon or dark entity removal, telling them they were not connected to their highest guidance, or being expected to answer the age-old question, "Is he going to call me?" Because I knew that I could always hear my guidance at the time of the sessions, I asked that there would only be previews when necessary. There was no need for me to stress about it ahead of time, since I had the reassurance that I would always be able to handle what was brought to me.

Forty-five minutes before the end of my work day, I was in the middle of reorganizing my office, and everything was in disarray when a married couple and their teenage son arrived. Gauging the nature of the lower energy that I could feel connected to them, I estimated that, under normal circumstances, I could have used two hours to work with them, but I only had forty-five minutes available before I needed to be home. The son, reluctant to speak or make eye contact with me, sat slumped in a chair. His mother explained that at a point in the past when her son was experiencing a similar dark time, she had taken him to a psychic healer outside of the country, who had been referred to her by a family member. The healer removed a dark entity from him and had done some other energy work. This seemed to have helped, but now, some time later, his mother realized that he needed someone closer by to help him with his sensitivity to energy and spirits. He had suffered some difficult relationships and was currently in a tough place according to her. His father sat on the couch and said very little. (I later learned that the only reason that he put any faith in me was that I offered my assistance without asking for payment.)

We worked to reestablish the young man's energetic

connection to God. I asked him to picture a cord of white Light that connected his crown chakra on the top of his head directly to Source. I can tell energetically when a person has connected and could feel something blocking him. I told him that it was his birthright to have that connection and to use whatever means to get through it. He powered through the obstruction and made his connection. I explained that he could allow that loving healing Light to fall on him, cleansing all lower vibrations and frustrations away.

We found a place in his energy field where he was upset with himself for sending negativity to others through his thoughts and actions. He needed to allow himself to forgive so that he could move forward. Sitting in this self-punishment was not a productive place for him. His mother helped him to forgive himself so that I could help him release the entities that were draining his energy. We did this in layers as quickly as I could so that I could leave on time to be home with my kids.

The hardest part was to get him to realize that he was worthy of God's love and forgiveness. He easily asked for forgiveness from those he felt he had wronged, but forgiving himself was the hardest thing for him to do. We released an elemental-type spirit from the Faerie Realm from his heart chakra. She had been there for a while and had managed get herself trapped in his aura. Her name was Lucy, and the young man had been speaking with her for some time. She found her bearings and returned to her own dimension.

We talked about his past and the dark energies he feared. I explained that he is safe and protected at all times. We quickly were able to work on his God/Source connection and to ask God for guidance about the entities he was unsure of. The goal of all of my contacts is to get others to receive their own answers for their highest good from God/Source. Since he was going to be connecting with beings and energies from other dimensions,

I knew that being able to get his own answers was the key to progress for him. He had been sensitive to other dimensions and his guides since he was a child. Soon he and his parents were on their way out of my office because I had to leave, and as they went, I told him to, "Stay in the Light."

In the next month I saw the young man on a regular basis. He made progress at an amazing pace. He was handling the complex energy cases that I handle, and I had to stay centered even when I knew he was at his limit and was scared. This was a field training position that I never thought I would be managing. Part of what his energy did was to remove the lower vibrations that did not belong. He has many other gifts, but those were the energies we were to learn first. There is no way to write a guidebook on how to handle each complicated energetic case, and that is why you need a way to communicate with Source in order to be able to know how to handle new energies.

I checked in, as I always do, to make sure that helping him was in my highest good, because it was like being on call at all times. Yes, I was told that I had agreed to help before I came into this lifetime. Yes, a valid contract with a member of my soul group. This was the first person I had come into contact with who was even more sensitive than I am. I am glad that I was able to have an understanding husband when I was learning quickly on my own. Many days were spent with the unknown and learning felt like I had been thrown in the middle of a huge mess and expected to find my way out on my own. This is the way I have always learned the best. I had not been aware of spirit when I was young, and I could not imagine what it must be like for a nineteen-year-old college student to learn at this rate while trying to find out who he is and what he came here to accomplish. I give him credit for an extremely difficult way to learn. I have had the time to learn who I am and to learn enough about love and life to feel there is a balance for me. This is something that he is still learning and will be learning for a long time. I am also glad that I learned as fast as I did so that I could be ready to help in this situation.

This is the situation that also made me that realize there is a need for me to write about the experiences so that others, young, old, and in-between, can have some knowledge to help them get through the scary and uneasy times that energy and spiritual work can bring. How many people are there who are not comfortable in their own lives because no one has helped them to realize they are not crazy, and they are left wondering whether there are ways to feel secure and to accomplish what they came here to do? It does not have to be scary.

I have worked with many psychic (aware of their connection to God/Source) children from before birth to teenagers. The commonality with them is to keep that communication with God/Source open and for them to learn at their own pace. They are very aware and will work and speak to their spirit guides from birth. They all fascinate me because they are all different. I do not classify them as Indigo, Crystal, etc. because there are too many varieties. I have seen some who able to get help on homework and during school from their God connection. They have the ability to change and heal their surroundings. Some are healing the planet when they aren't even aware that they have that type of power. Some of them are here to help all of us learn to connect higher and to bring the Light into our lives.

They are often aware of dense energies, and if allowed to grow, will see that the Light of God/Creator/Source works through them to change the density of the current worldly paradigm in which we live. They do not need other psychic children to grow. That would be like letting all of our Inner Children play together and pick up ideas from each other. My suggestion is to let God teach them and let them become aware in their own time. If anything, the parents are the ones who may need to connect with other trustworthy spiritual guidance, to help them realize that they are fully equipped to raise their children. All they really need are love and the opportunity to grow at their own pace.

Energy Vampires

Energy vampires were at one time outside my belief system, but when a client claimed that he was one, I read a book on the subject that taught, among other things, how to "feed" on the energy of others without their consent. The author rationalized that darkness served a purpose in our world. When I inquired about this, God clearly communicated that this line of thinking saddened Him, and that there is no place for darkness in the pure vibration of love, which exists without anything else. Love is. If someone suggests that you embrace darkness, it is another trick-of-the-trade. Energy vampires are not comfortable with the energy of pure love, so they derive their energy from others instead of through a connection to God/Spirit.

I was holding a spiritual class at my office when a young woman chose to sit in everyone's energy and take from those in the room who were weak and unprotected. I was very aware of what was going on and questioned her about it. She explained that she did this at psychic fairs and at other public places as a means of amusement. She would also see what people were hiding, and she enjoyed this connection with people. In another instance, I observed a man attempt to obtain energy from a young lady who was suffering from mental illness. He gained access to her energy through the loophole of a joint past life. I have also seen people claiming to be healers who, for their own pleasure, enter into the energetic sexual space of their clients. I am aware of "top notch" teachers who misdirect their students to places and professions that keep them from reaching their goals. Some siphon off the power from others' destinies in order to fuel their own abilities. The "I must be the best" mentality hinders professional psychics and healers who have come here to help the planet.

I have often wondered why they choose the darkness over the Light. When you connect to the Light, that vibration of love wants you to feel it at all levels of your being. If you have an area that you are healing from this lifetime such as old hurts, trauma, or other painful memories that are stored, they are brought to the surface for you to look at and heal. After you find peace and forgiveness, you allow this painful part to be transformed to Light. Being Light allows for you to be the clearest channel for the God/Source/Healing energy this planet needs. Say, *"I choose to own my power and Light from this point, into all directions, into eternity."* When this is said, you are energetically protected by the very highest part of yourself, that part of us that is God/Source.

Stealing Someone's Spiritual Destiny

Sometimes I am amazed by the way people hurt one another, especially in the spiritual realm where we are Lightworkers and should be promoting peace. One of the enemy's game plans is to infiltrate the places Lightworkers congregate with the means to take another's soul destiny. They may appear to be a kind, caring spiritual seeker or teacher, but the energy they ground here is of the dark. I had experience with this firsthand.

I opened up quickly in this lifetime and had a purpose to help missing people and to voice the truth on spiritual matters. I had no previous knowledge of the metaphysical or mediums. All I knew was that I needed information about how to speak to and help people who were deceased. I located a nearby metaphysical shop that offered a set of classes to teach mediumship. I booked a reading and was really nervous but excited to finally have answers on how to offer assistance to the missing person whose spirit had been around me. This "spiritual teacher," who had credentials in metaphysical work and over twenty years of knowledge, was going to help me. When I sat down she said she could tell that I was nervous. She had me hold her hands. I said that I needed help with missing persons and asked if she could give me some direction. It was at that moment that she accessed my spiritual destiny and made it her own. I had no idea that the power of my spiritual destiny and identity had been hijacked until several years later when I got to the point where I am able to have an awareness of such things.

The ability to expand your awareness requires that you open your paradigm to be able to see things that you didn't know existed. I once thought that destiny was exactly that—destiny that you would easily get to because it was yours. Spiritual destiny is the reason you have for coming to the planet when you are of God and Light. You come here to change the way people feel about God/Source and to help them know that there can be peace. If the other team can access and take that from you, you will never find your path. Some of us can break through these barriers, and our mission is to help others, when they are blocked or stuck, to do the same.

Some individuals consciously or subconsciously feel that they have a proprietary claim on certain areas of energy work. I have felt the resisting energies from them when working with clients who have previously used their services or attended their classes, when charging or programming items, or when writing my own information about crystals for which they think that they have already written the definitive word. They think that they own you and your gifts. When you try to do something similar to what they do with you, but in another setting or with other people, they are jealous and their energy can try to block you. While disconnecting a line of energy from a local shaman to a friend and myself, this type of energy disrupted the spiritual work my friend and I were doing. The shaman did not want the work of assisting Earthbound Souls in crossing to the Light to be done without being a part of it.

Filters can also be placed on your spiritual destiny. "You will never succeed; you will never make money; you need someone else to teach you; life is meant to be hard; you are not meant to have inner vision." Statements like these can cause you to doubt yourself and never see who you are. In some cases they place a false destiny in your path, sending you another direction. I went five years without knowing this had happened, but I do now and am sharing with you so you that can undo this if you are locked in anything similar. And, yes, multiple people can hijack the same person for related reasons. I have had a client with more than ten different people accessing her power.

To remove filters and anything else that is blocking you, first "center yourself in love," then move to the 9th Dimension with the intent to escape the binds placed upon you and your soul. Ask Source to bless you in your path and destiny, and then fly. Go do what you came here to do. Change this planet into what it once "was and will be" again someday, a place of love and peace.

Curses and Intentions

I had a hypnotherapy session for weight loss from a partner in my business at that time. Afterward, I found that I had more cravings for sweets than before, and I wanted to find out why the session had not worked. I later learned that during this session my partner's subconscious thoughts about ideal weight and strategy for weight loss, rather than the stated intentions of the hypnosis, had become trapped in my subconscious. The person was not on my side and had placed a harmful intention—a curse to fail—in my subconscious.

Some people do this intentionally. An older man came into my office for a reading one evening. He brought a "gift" of water charged with a "vibration of healing" similar to the Rife machine. I placed the two gallons of water with stickers on them on a shelf in my office. I started the reading by asking what had brought him to me, and he answered, "I want to see how good a psychic you are." And from there he began asking general questions about patents and gaming licenses. I asked him what was in the list of questions that he had on a specific page in his notebook. He explained that he was looking for the price of gold and when it would reach a certain price point. He divulged that he had placed psychics under hypnosis to get the information about the prices of gold and silver without having their consent for that line of questioning. I decided to ask this man to leave after learning about his overstepping and what he had come to find out. He left but insisted on leaving the water. I quickly detected that the water was charged to harm in the event that the energy between he and I was broken. People who leave you gifts and expect something from you in return have energy similar to a curse. If you believe in curses or hexes, then it is possible to place one on you. Don't stop accepting gifts; just know that if you are sensitive to energy, you may feel this when someone is expecting something or holding out conditions related to giving you an item.

Enochian Healing and Removal Symbols

Dense, demonic, or other non-beneficial energy, such as thought forms (ideas or emotions) and residual energy, can be lifted from a person, place, or object by using the following symbols. The origin of these symbols is Enochian, which is the original Angel language. They were received through my connection with the Angelic Realm, which allows me to access these and many other manuscripts to assist us with ascension and determine the spiritual truth of the history and future of this planet. Moving forward sometimes requires an adjustment to how we see reality and answers revealed over time to what was previously hidden.

Always start from a place of love and not fear. Center yourself in love. Symbolize love by drawing two vertical lines (looks like 11). Picture yourself between the lines.

Vay-Te-Se /vay-tay-say/, **"Release the Hold"**

For those of you who feel energy, curses are located in the solar plexus and connect with the Will Center of that chakra. Curses feel restrictive and can be seen as the color blue in the solar plexus with an appearance similar to a disc if you are clairvoyant. The more you fight the energy, the better hold it takes in the chakra. Place one hand over the heart chakra and one over the sacral chakra simultaneously. After a minute or two the energy will fill the area with Light. Use the symbol for **Vay-Te-Se** over each chakra. Either visualize the symbol or draw it with your hand over each chakra. This symbol separates the energy from both the sender and receiver in all space time possibilities.

I-Se-Dente, "Saving Grace" /ee-say-doan-tay/
[Note: "Den" spelling, but long O vowel pronunciation]

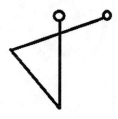

Demonic energy can reside with a person or location. Demonic energy attached to a person will connect at the person's solar plexus chakra, and the color will be seen by clairvoyants as a black mass with red edges or as the energy presents itself. It will cover and use the person's spiritual connection point on the left hip area as its energy supply. First use the symbol **I-Se-Dente** and either visualize or draw it with your hand over the third eye, root chakra, and bottom of both feet. Place one hand on the throat chakra and the other over the higher heart chakra.

Preserve the love vibration originally created in each and all living things with the **I-Se-Dente** symbol, which cleans in all space time possibilities simultaneously.

Es-tu /es-too/, **"Only Love"**

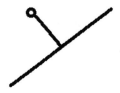

Es-Ta-Me-Tu /es-tah-may-too/, **"One with God"**

To protect the vulnerable, mentally ill or disabled, use the **Es-Tu** symbol on the left side of the head and neck. This is a susceptible place for those with mental disabilities. Either visualize the symbol or draw it above these areas with your hand. Place your hands on the higher heart and throat chakra and fill the energy of the person or place you are working on with Light. Finally, place the **Es-Ta-Me-Tu** symbol, either visually or by drawing with your hand, over the root chakra.

Ban and clear Fallen Angels and other beasts and do general clearing and banning of lower and disruptive energies with the symbols **Es-tu** and **Es-ta-Me-Tu**.

Es-Ma-Ta-Ra /es-mah-tah-rah/, "All that is Holy within Us"

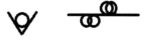

Do healing on all levels with the symbol **Es-Ma-Ta-Ra** symbol.

Deactivation Codes

When someone else's jealousy or greed is a force trying to stop you from doing your work in the Light, you can use a numerical deactivation code to close the door on that energy. Each code represents the energy needed to deactivate the illusion of division. These numbers are connected to "all that is and will be" at levels of which the human mind is unaware. The divisive jealousy/greed drama is actually a program to keep Lightworkers in a state of chaos and discontent. It is stored in the subconscious of the solar plexus chakra and is activated when one is fully in their power and entering their spiritual destiny and the work they came here to accomplish. To try to make you believe that this discordant energy belongs to you, it will mask itself as a familiar loop of emotional or spiritual discontent that you have already healed or are in the process of healing.

Read or look at the number sequences:
Deactivate the false program of jealousy/greed and division.
601 21 444 6674117
If you break it down, **601** represents free will, **21** represents the Inner Child, **444** is a general clearing code, and **6674117** represents a looping of discontent patterns. I have used this to get to the root of the hidden Free Will pattern just by saying the number out loud to a client.

> **Reconnect** to who you are, as a soul with a strong bond to God/Source, when things pull you away and you just can't seem to get the connection back yourself (Connection to your Higher Self).
>
> 189 74 77 8 9

> **Clear** any stubborn blocks in the subconscious or conscious mind and any entity.
>
> (Underlined numbers are repeating.)
>
> 111211111163 77 11121 0009 335 789 444 7789 601 444 66 7789 11121 0009 1112<u>3</u> <u>082</u> 7789

Source/Creator will be giving us additional patterns of advanced numerical codes at a higher level, and I will publish more information in the future as I receive and document it.

> "Believe that things will turn out as they should. Love those that can't see things as you do. Find love for those that are most difficult to love right now. Believe that there is good in all regardless of what it feels like. Open your heart, even when it hurts. Try again with open eyes. We are always here. You are not alone. We feel with you. Love is the answer; it always will be. Long ago it was the answer and it still is today."
>
> —Archangel Gabriel on behalf of the Archangels

Testimonials

In a deeply stressful time in my life, I was guided to a healing session with Diana. Even though I wasn't familiar with Diana or her expertise at that time, somehow I knew that I needed her help. I was filled with such deep despair after experiencing the sudden deaths of people close to me that I could barely function in my daily life. I spent the afternoon before my appointment in tears, severe anxiety, and overwhelming grief.

When I met Diana, I remembered her asking me what I wanted to work on in the session. I told her I wanted to be more at peace and less sad about my losses. She had me lay down on the table, and she started putting crystals around me and on different parts of my body. The anxiety quickly left my body and left me feeling very relaxed and comfortable. As Diana spoke, used the crystals, and integrated other healing techniques during the session, I could sense her genuine compassion, insightfulness, and connectedness to a divine source. As the heaviness from my body was releasing, I felt a warm, loving, supportive energy wrapping itself around me and filling me with peace and lightness. Near the end of the session, I was instantly awakened by the midsection of my body being lifted off the table slightly but enough to know that "something" was pulled out of my body. Diana's hands did not touch me at all during this session, so I was a little alarmed at the sensation; however, very quickly and ever so gently a warm tingly lightness surrounded this area below my ribs and the same peaceful cocooning energy was filling this area and sealing any open, raw wounds. This experience is undeniably the strongest healing force I have ever experienced.

After the session, Diana took some time to talk about the experience. I left her feeling relaxed and peaceful with renewed strength and balance that I hadn't had in at least a couple years prior to this session. I don't have the words to express my gratitude for Diana and the healing work she provides. All I know is I was close to an emotional breakdown before I discovered her, and I now have been able to fully move forward from the pain of my losses to a more peaceful and fulfilling life.

My experience with Diana has been ongoing and dimensional. Things you may not believe in or know about can happen. With her, I have had many experiences with removing demons and fallen angels. As I continue to raise my vibration, they exist at different levels of those vibrations and try to hold me at that level. The more I raised my vibration, the more my spiritual knowledge and gifts would increase. When I released these blocks, beliefs, or dimensional dark entities, which had attached to me, I would become more aware of the spiritual life. I could sense and feel more of what was going on around me in spirit form. Removing beliefs that don't serve you or separate you from God is what I have been learning thru all my experiences.

Many times I had to text Diana, and she could take care of my situation from wherever she was, and then return a text to let me know what was going on. I didn't believe in fallen angels until I was attacked by many while trying to help a friend who ended up being a fallen angel himself.

I started feeling a sharp pain in my back muscles and joints. It felt like long claws stabbing in two spots with a heavy weight at the same time. This was just after I was teaching my friend to feel good and be happy about himself. My friend was getting better and was learning to be more aware of his thoughts. While talking to him, I was able to see three dark entities around him, with my 3rd eye. When I first felt this pain, I thought it might be from those dark entities. After texting Diana to see what she could feel, she texted back saying they were actually fallen angels.

This went on all morning, and I knew it wasn't a normal feeling, something outside of me was happening. I was in a quiet place where I could close my eyes and meditate. I saw a couple of them and could feel/sense them more. She asked my permission to remove them. She told me that feeling would be gone in about 5 minutes. Sure enough it was gone. This happened several times over the next few days. I then realized this was coming from my friend and the fallen angels didn't want me to help him anymore.

Diana is a healer's healer, who is often called upon to sort out discordant energies. Like a conductor directing an orchestra, she leads groups of experienced and novice energy workers—balancing, listening, drawing out, always aware of the whole. She follows her path and sometimes "does it afraid" when she does not know the outcome or when the truth that she reveals is difficult for some to hear. She has developed at an amazing pace and is continually evolving. Diana displays a rare generosity and lack of ego in her desire to help others connect and realize who they are and why they're here.

Being empathic can have its advantages and disadvantages. I was being overwhelmed by a depressive and hopeless energy that I knew was not mine. I tried several techniques that I have used in the past to release myself from these types of psychic attacks, but I could not free myself from this one. It seemed too large and too much for me to handle. I contacted Diana and told her what was going on, and she was able to clear the psychic attack and the feelings of overwhelming dread that were being sent to me. During Diana's energetic clearing, I physically experienced nausea, headache, and my whole body started shaking. With Diana's intervention, it felt as if a waterfall was being poured over me, rinsing away any way this could attach to me and also washing away any residual energies that may have remained. It took about 20 minutes or so to feel completely at peace. I was later gifted the validation of divine intervention by being surrounded by a bunch of little white butterflies. Your accuracy and insight into energetic ties is nothing short of amazing! Thank you, Diana, for helping me with your intuitiveness and healing powers.

CPSIA information can be obtained at www.ICGtesting.com
Printed in the USA
LVOW05s0627191113

361810LV00001B/5/P